I am the GREATEST

50 Ways to Ignite
Your Passion,
Power and Purpose
to Get More Out
of Business and Life!

KAREN PHELPS

Phelps
Positive
Performance

karenphelps.com

Published by Phelps Positive Performance Inc., Clarkston, Michigan.

Printed in The United States of America

ISBN 978-0-9828586-0-8

Disclaimer – The purpose of this book it to educate and entertain. The author or publisher does not guarantee that anyone following the techniques, suggestions, tips and ideas will become successful. The author or publisher shall have neither liability or responsibility to anyone with respect to any loss or damage caused, or alleged to be caused, directly or indirectly by the information contained in this book.

www.karenphelps.com   www.attitudetools.com   www.karenspeaking.com

Positive
Performance

Cover and book designed by Anthony J. Fisher, Freelance Artist, Inc.
FishFreelance @aol.com   FishFryToon.com

KAREN PHELPS *America's "Can Do Attitude" Speaker*

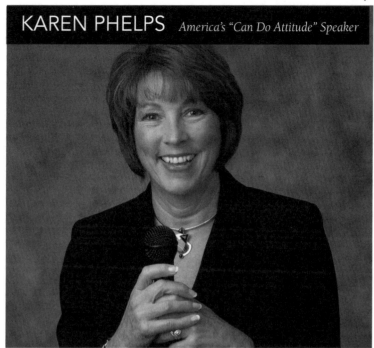

A few Words of Motivation and Inspiration:

1. When confronted with a problem you have one of two choices to make. You can find an excuse for the problem or find a way to solve it. Just remember the choice is yours.

2. Life is what happens to you when you think you've got it altogether!

3. The difference between "thinkers and doers?" The size of their bank account. You can think about making a lot of money as much as you want but YOU HAVE TO DO SOMETHING ABOUT IT to change your circumstances! That, my friend, is the SECRET!

4. Love like there is no tomorrow!

5. You "CAN DO" anything if you want it bad enough to work for it!! Nothing happens without action!

The Ideal Speaker for Your Next Event!

To schedule Karen to Speak at your Event:

Call: **248-625-4897**

or

Email: **Support@Karenphelps.com**

Check Out These Other Resources from Karen Phelps:

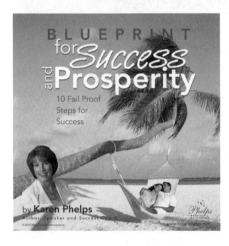

Blueprint for Success and Prosperity – provides fun and easy methods to increase your success in your business and personal life in fast order…so you can skyrocket your accomplishments!

Complete System Includes: 3 DVDs, 3 CDs and Binder

Blueprint for Mastering Direct Selling Leadership – How to Make Big Bucks – provides a complete step-by-step program for building a dynamic direct sales organization.

Complete System Includes: 8 DVDs, 10 CDs, Binder and Data Template CD

For Direct Sellers who want the edge over their competition visit:
www.directsellingdoctor.com

Plus these are just a few of the many other items available individually or in sets:

It's a Party Out There –
Action Guide, DVD and CDs

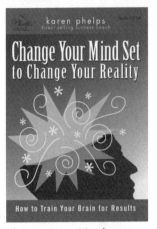

Change Your Mindset to Change Your Reality – *CD*

Excelling in Direct Selling
– CD

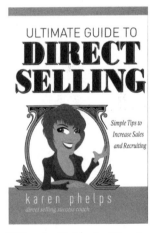

Ultimate Guide to Direct Selling - Book

For more information or to order any of these products visit
www.karenphelps.com/shop.html

About Karen Phelps

Karen Phelps has delivered motivational presentations at conferences and conventions worldwide. Her performances not only captivate and motivate the audience they inspire attendees to take action to becoming better in all areas of their life.

Having spent 25 years in direct selling as a top seller and leader, she knows what it takes to get to the top and stay there. Through personal and team sales achievements, including several #1 positions, Karen earned every company trip while she was in direct selling traveling to over 20 worldwide destinations.

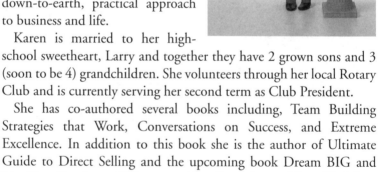

Her powerful message of becoming better than you ever thought possible is something she not only shares with the audience, but is how she lives her life! Karen is a constant student, unafraid of taking on the next challenge. Audiences are mesmerized by her down-to-earth, practical approach to business and life.

Karen is married to her high-school sweetheart, Larry and together they have 2 grown sons and 3 (soon to be 4) grandchildren. She volunteers through her local Rotary Club and is currently serving her second term as Club President.

She has co-authored several books including, Team Building Strategies that Work, Conversations on Success, and Extreme Excellence. In addition to this book she is the author of Ultimate Guide to Direct Selling and the upcoming book Dream BIG and Live Your Destiny – 10 Secrets to Stop Surviving and Start Thriving.

To sign up for Free Motivational and Direct Selling newsletters visit www.karenphelps.com

Chapters

Take a RISK

It's scary out in the real world and every day we are faced with choices. Are YOU always making the "Safe Choice?" It takes courage to leave the land of mediocrity! It takes courage to risk losing it all because you have a great idea!

Mother Teresa took a risk when she began working with the poor. Walt Disney took a risk when he began constructing Disneyland. Muhammad Ali took a risk when after a long absence he started fighting again.

All of these people…plus many more can say, "I AM THE GREATEST!"

> "He who is not courageous enough to take risks will accomplish nothing in life."
> ~Muhammad Ali

2

Dream BIG!

Don't be afraid to DREAM BIG for you never know what is waiting for you around the corner. Without dreams your life can be very boring! With dreams you continue to live life on the edge trying things you have never done before, taking risks, accepting challenges and living with passion. WOW! It sounds great just thinking about it!

Your dreams are a very important part of your life! Your visions of who you want to become, what you want to have, who you want to be surrounded by must be played and replayed in your mind before they are realized in your life. Your dreams and visions become the foundation upon which your goals are based! BIG dreams help you set bigger goals!

It is time to DREAM BIG again! You can earn $10,000, $50,000, $100,000 or more each year! But you will never reach $100,000 when you only dream about $10,000! What do you want? Do you want a vacation home? Do you want to remodel your current home? Do you want to have a college fund for your children? WHAT DO YOU WANT?

Big Dreams Change the World! Become a Big Dreamer NOW!

"Go confidently in the direction of your dreams and live the life you have imagined."
~Eleanor Roosevelt

3

Create your PLAN!

There is no dream too Big for you as long as you have an action plan!

Where do you start? With the end of course! Once you know the specific result you are after you must know how to reach it. Close your eyes and picture yourself in your dream! You have accomplished what you wanted to accomplish and you are celebrating your success.

Now look back along the way and you will discover the steps you needed to take to make your dreams come true! Hurry and write those steps down! You have just created your action plan so keep it with you always!

Start with a picture of your goals as already achieved in the future, and work back to the present. Imagine the steps you would have taken to get from where you are now to where you want to be.

~Brian Tracy

4

Decide WHO You Want to Become

Life is not just about what you can acquire but about who you become in the process.

If you take time to plan not only what you want to have but also who you want to become you will begin to work on yourself as a person.

As YOU pursue each new dream you will begin to do things you never dreamed you were capable of and you will become a person who is now actively participating in life rather than sitting on the sidelines.

"The big challenge is to become all that you have the possibility of becoming. You cannot believe what it does to the human spirit to maximize your human potential and stretch yourself to the limit."

~Jim Rohn

5

Watch Out for Bumps & Potholes Along the Way!

The true test of someone's character is how they handle obstacles along the way!

If you live in an area that gets hard frost & snow followed by thawing, refreezing and then thawing again you probably have roads that are filled with potholes until the repair crew comes and fixes them. You always need to keep your eyes on the road and do your best to go around the potholes or you risk doing severe damage to your car.

Such is your quest for success. Obstacles will appear when you least expect them and all you can do is keep your eyes on the goal, make a little adjustment in your plan and continue on your way!

"A pessimist sees the difficulty in every opportunity; an Optimist sees the opportunity in every difficulty."

~Sir Winston Churchill

6

Become a Champion in Everything You Do!

Once you begin your journey you will be amazed at the changes in you. You will begin to do things you never dreamed of doing. You will begin to accomplish small goals along the way. You will begin to push yourself because you know you can. Each small accomplishment provides you with enough fuel to take the next step!

When you attempt anything, give it your all! Give 100% to everything you set out to do and the CHAMPION hidden within YOU will come out. So don't hold back, give it all you got!

"A champion is someone who surpasses personal limits. You are never given a dream without also being given the power to make them come true."

~Richard Bach
US Olympics

7

Don't Lose Sight of Your Dreams

Create a vision board of your dreams and goals and keep it in front of you all the time! NOTHING can stop a person who keeps their eyes on their goal.

Although he had one failing business venture after another in his lifetime, Walt Disney never gave up hope that his dreams would one day be realized. When Disney created Snow White and the Seven Dwarfs, he almost went under again financially. In fact, when Disney was borrowing money he had to show why this film was going to dominate the industry by being the first feature film of its time complete with sound and Technicolor. Upon its release, with many claiming that it would be the end of Disney, the film grossed over 7 million dollars, or in today's figures, well over 95 million dollars profit. Be like Walt Disney and never give up on your dreams.

"Cherish your own vision and your dreams as they are the children of your soul; the blueprints of your ultimate achievements."
~Napoleon Hill

8

Tough It Out!

There's a saying over the desk in my library I had made after my mom passed way that had been her quote from her senior yearbook, "She can because she BELIEVES she can!" I am reminded everyday what I can accomplish when I believe!

If everything came easily you would probably get bored and toss the idea aside. If you ask a successful person what the keys to their success were, everyone would undoubtedly have many different answers. Most everyone would say they had an ability to "stay the course" and to persevere when they wanted to give up!

If it is worthwhile and you want it bad enough you will find a way to make it happen! BELIEVE!

"Life is not easy for any of us. But what of that? We must have perseverance and, above all, confidence in ourselves. We must believe that we are gifted for something, and that this something, at whatever cost, must be attained."

~Madame Curie

9

Try Something New

I watched the video of an eighty year old woman who went skydiving for the first time because it was on her "bucket list" of things to do before she died! Exhilarated she explained how excited she was each time she tried something new. I believe it is keeping her young!

That doesn't mean you have to go jumping out of air-planes but before you say NO to the next new thing, take a few minutes to think about it and ask yourself how excited would you be when you can tell your friends, "I DID IT!"

"Twenty years from now you will be more disappointed by the things that you didn't do than by the ones you did do."

~Mark Twain

10

Always Talk Positively to Yourself

It is ten times easier for someone to believe something negative about them than it is to believe something positive. YOU must get some positive thought waves going into your brain. You must train your brain to believe and the easiest way to do it is to repeat mantras over and over again.

I remember watching Muhammad Ali on television when I was young. When he was being interviewed he kept telling everyone how great he was. I was mesmerized because I had never seen anyone in my life who had ever displayed so much confidence.

Begin today with simple mantras like, "I am the greatest _____." (Salesperson, leader, mother, husband, teacher, etc)

Or my Tony Robbins favorite, "Day by day I'm getting better in every way."

"I am the greatest; I said that even before I knew I was."
~ Muhammad Ali

"It's the repetition of affirmations that leads to belief. And once that belief becomes a deep conviction, things begin to happen. "
~Muhammad Ali

11

When You Think You Can Go No Further – Keep Going

Anyone who watched the 2008 Summer Olympics observed history in the making as Michaels Phelps took home 8 Gold Medals in swimming.

The 400 Individual Medley is one of the most grueling races for a swimmer, who swims 4 laps each with a different stroke. It was by far one of Michael's best races as he posted a world record time. He accomplished this by going faster in the back length than he did in the first which doesn't work for most people.

Most races are won or lost in the final lap which is where you have to be mentally and physically strong and push yourself like never before! So when you think you cannot go any further, when you are ready to give up – KEEP GOING!

"No matter how dark things seem to be or actually are, raise your sights and see the possibilities – always see them, for they're always there."

~Norman Vincent Peale

Lose Graciously

Competition can bring out the best and the worst in people. There are clips of teams who have just lost an important game who are so bitter about the loss they go on and on about the injustice of it all. It was the referee's fault, it was another player's fault, it was the coach's fault and on and on and on!

They are poor losers who don't understand the importance of losing graciously!

Then there are losers who understand EVERYONE loses some and it is best not to dwell, blame, rant and rave about it BUT instead toss it aside and move forward.

Focus on how to win next time by analyzing what you could have done differently or better and next time you'll be back in the winner's circle!

"I never thought of losing, but now that it's happened, the only thing is to do it right. That's my obligation to all the people who believe in me. We all have to take defeats in life."

~Muhammad Ali

13

Done is Better than Perfect

Does your quest for perfection prevent you from getting started on a new project or from completing a task? There are doers and then there are "let me think about the best way to do this" people who wait for everything to be in perfect alignment before they begin.

Perfectionism must be overcome before you will ever begin to relentlessly pursue your dreams. You must be willing to begin as best you can without hesitation and without waiting.

"Quit waiting for perfection! You can't study perfection; you keep doing it until it becomes improved over time!"

~Karen Phelps

14

Avoid Playing
the Blame Game

It's always difficult when things don't go as planned to discover the real reason behind what went wrong. We often look for someone else to blame. When we become defensive about something it is most often because we know in our heart that we could have done something different to get a different result.

One of the hardest things you will ever do is learn to move forward to the next project without giving any excuses to yourself. One's need to justify the previous outcome will often prevent him or her from discovering the solution to the problem.

Work hard on finding a better way the next time around!

"When confronted with a problem you have one of two choices to make. You can find an excuse for the problem or find a way to solve it. Ultimately the choice is yours."

~Karen Phelps

15

Find the Champion in YOU!

Do you remember the first time you did something you never thought you could do? Do you remember how great you felt? Do you remember what you had to go through to get there? You most likely had to dig down deep inside you to create a vision of what could be.

I remember the first time I set a goal to be a #1 achiever with my sales company. The same night I had set the goal for myself I had a dream about being #1. The dream was crystal clear to me and I was on stage with a crown on my head, a #1 banner across my body and a dozen long-stemmed roses in my hand. When I awoke the next morning I KNEW I would be #1 the following year. The vision stayed with me until I made it happen.

Create a vision of what you want and think about it often especially when things aren't going as planned.

"Champions aren't made in the gym. Champions are made from something deep inside them; a desire, a dream, and a vision."
~Muhammad Ali

Don't Give Up

My house sits at the top of a steep hill and when I return from a long bike ride and face that hill I am always tempted to get off and walk my bike up the driveway! In fact, when we first moved in I began bike riding and when my ride was over and I arrived at the bottom of our driveway I would get off and walk the bike up.

One morning I decided to try to ride it up. I looked at the top of the hill and thought to myself, "I can't do this." Sure enough, half-way up I got off and walked the bike the rest of the way up. The next morning I tried a different approach. When I got to the end of the road I kept my eyes focused on my front tire and kept repeating my favorite "Little Engine that Could" phrase, "I know I can, I know I can" and before I knew it I was at the top of the driveway.

I never looked at the hill the same way again. Now no matter how tired I am when I return from my ride, I know with a little more effort I'll reach my destination.

No matter how tired you are, DON'T GIVE UP!

It isn't the mountains ahead to climb that wear you out; it's the pebble in your shoe.
~Muhammad Ali

17

Stop Procrastinating and GET IT DONE!

Many people are so overwhelmed by the task at hand that it takes days, weeks or months to begin a task. Procrastination is putting off what needs to be done sooner or later and the sooner you get to it the better YOU WILL FEEL!

When you know a project needs to get done and you avoid working on it sooner or later you'll begin having a nagging feeling in the pit of your stomach because a deadline is approaching, or has already passed and you sink deeper and deeper into a hole.

I wear a bracelet that I received as a gift from James Malinchak that says, "Get things done fast" so I am reminded to begin and complete everything at the fastest pace possible. When I avoid doing things I have a nagging feeling in my stomach BUT every time I begin and finish a task I have a great feeling of accomplishment!

What is the difference between "thinkers and doers?" It is the size of their bank account.

You can think about making a lot of money as much as you want but YOU HAVE TO DO SOMETHING ABOUT IT to change your circumstances! That my friend is the "Secret"

"The only thing that will move you closer to your goals is ACTION!"

~Karen Phelps

18

Every Failure is a New Opportunity

After Thomas Edison's family was told by his teacher that he had a learning disability and was too dumb to learn, his mother decided to home-school him. As a young man, he was broke and starving in New York when he happened upon a brokerage firm manager who was in a panic because the "stock-ticker" had broken down. Tom fixed it and was hired on the spot for $300 per month, twice the going rate of an electrician. A while later he received $40,000 for his rights to a new "stock-ticker" which was the first time he had received payment for an invention.

He had been working on a way to transmit the human voice and was bitterly disappointed when Alexander Graham Bell did so before him. His desire to beat his competition caused him to invent the incandescent light bulb and then the first economically viable system of generating light and heat to the masses. He continued to work on inventions introducing the Kinetiscope to create motion pictures, the Dictaphone, and the mimeograph machine and he founded the Edison General Electric Co.

He obtained his 1,093rd and last patent at the age of 83 and he is considered one of the most influential people of the millennium. The most amazing thing of all was he did all of this AFTER someone told him he was too dumb to learn!

"Only a man who knows what it is like to be defeated can reach down to the bottom of his soul and come up with the extra ounce of power it takes to win when the match is even."
~Muhammad Ali

19

Continually Ask Yourself..."What If?"

The imagination plays a powerful part in our life as we are growing up. As small children we played with our toys and lived in a land of make believe. Boys often believe they are super heroes ready to save the world, while small girls live in their fantasy castle with beautiful dresses and Prince Charming, of course!

Then we grow up! Our imagination begins to disappear along with our dreams. We become adolescents and then adults and we follow what everyone else is doing rather than dare to imagine, what if I did it differently?

Begin today to look at everything from a different perspective. Use your imagination to create fabulous fairy tales in your mind. Place yourself in the center of the story. It is often the process of really expanding our imagination that we find solutions to problems, answers to questions and dreams that are waiting to be acted on!

> *"The man who has no imagination has no wings."*
>
> ~Muhammad Ali

20

Give it Your Best Shot

Once you make a commitment to something or someone you have to give 100%. Winners don't show up and
then put in minimal effort. Winners give it all they've got!
Winners play to win!

Think back to the times when you didn't give 100%.
How did you feel? Most likely you felt a nagging voice
deep inside that chastised you for not giving it your all!

It's easy to commit and say "yes" to things we really
don't want to do. Once that happens you will begin to
look for a way out and if there is no way out you will not
put in the amount of effort you need to succeed. Would
you be better off to say "no" if you don't have the time,
energy, skills or desire to give it your best? Ultimately the
choice is yours!

*"I play to win, whether during practice or a
real game. And I will not let anything get in
the way of me and my competitive enthusiasm to win."*

~Michael Jordan

21

Stay Focused

Cell phone, internet, Facebook, e-mails, texting, tweeting, posting and all other forms of interruptions create chaos in our life and help us to lose focus. Although many of them are minor disruptions often you can be moving toward your goal at a fairly good clip and then any disruption causes you to lose focus and it often takes much longer to get back on track. Do your best to avoid constant interruptions and you will find you get much more done!

When you are "in the zone" working to complete a project or training for an event you do everything within your power to avoid distractions. When I'm writing I close down the internet and my emails so I don't lose my train of thought which would result in lost time trying to get back to where I was before the interruption. Many people find it easy to close a door and hang a "do not disturb" sign outside when they need to stay centered on the task or project they are currently working on. Sure, it's not easy to do all the time, especially when you have children around but it is doable in many situations.

Focus will help you move through tasks quicker and with more efficiency. Staying focused will help you accomplish more in less time while you relentlessly pursue your dreams and goals!

"When I am focused, there is not one single thing or person that can stand in the way of my doing something."

~Michael Phelps
Olympic Gold Medalist

Do What Must be Done

Have you ever been in a situation where you knew something had to be done but you didn't want to do it! You probably procrastinated and put it off as long as possible but hopefully you finally got around to it! It's crucial to do the things that must be done even if you don't want to do them!

Within every job and opportunity there are tasks and thing that need to be done that we might not want to do. When we are in school we don't want to do homework and yet we know doing homework will help us get better grades. If you are in sales you don't want to make cold calls and yet we know we have to make calls to set appointments.

You'll often discover that doing the things you don't want to do will move you closer to your goals so that you can ultimately begin doing the things you want to do!

"You do the things you have to do, so you can do the things you want to do"
~From the movie "The Great Debaters"

23

Have FUN!

"Life's a Party and You're Invited!" Karen Phelps

The busier we get the less likely we are to take time off to just have fun! We may plan some time for fun family activities and then we take a good look at the house or garage that needs cleaning, the laundry that needs to be done, the lawn that needs to be mowed and on and on and on! Pretty soon our fun family outing day turns into another dull day doing the same old stuff!

My observations have been that no matter what happens everything will still be there when you get home! It's not going anywhere and often, having fun time re-energizes you and the family so when you get to the chores they get done faster!

Fun time can always be used as a reward to get kids to help out, just make sure you schedule it in at least weekly! Family game night, biking, walks in the park, cross-country skiing, ice-skating, roller skating, sailing, and swimming were just some of the things we did together as a family when our sons were growing up. These were special times, never to be forgotten. Lighten up and HAVE FUN!

"Having fun reduces stress and renews your body and spirit! Life is too short not to have fun!"

~Karen Phelps

24

Don't Quit!

We had a rule in our house that once you started something you had to finish it. So you had better be sure you wanted to try a new sport because once you signed up you had to complete the season so you didn't let your coach or your team down.

I remember the year my son Bryan wanted to play soccer. He signed up, went to the practices, played a few games and about 1/3 of the way into the season he let us know he didn't like playing soccer. No worries, we told him, you don't have to play next year but you have to finish out the season. It was a hard lesson to teach but after that he never joined anything unless he was absolutely sure it was what he wanted to do!

In many areas of our lives it is much easier to quit than it is to press on. The first time you quit on yourself you begin altering the pattern of your life. Then each new challenge brings another opportunity to quit. Pretty soon quitting becomes a habit and you realize it becomes more and more difficult to complete something.

Do everything you can possibly do before you quit! Don't let the quitting cycle begin!

"Once you learn to quit, it becomes a habit."
~Vince Lombardi

25

Have a Great Attitude

If you knew there was a magic pill you could take that would help you get more out of life you would surely want to know about it and most likely would be taking it, wouldn't you?

There is a magic pill that not only controls our thoughts but also our actions and that is our attitude. You'll find it is easier to expect good results when you have a good attitude. A positive attitude will help you look for solutions not more problems.

Over thirty years ago I invested in Zig Ziglar's "How to Stay Motivated" course and to this day I often use his technique when I wake up in the morning. Zig recommends jumping out of bed, slapping your hands together and saying, "It's going to be a great day!" It never ceases to amaze me that every time I do this I HAVE A GREAT DAY!

"The minute you begin to change your attitude is the minute YOU CAN begin to change your results."

~James Malinchak

26

Let Your Heart Guide You

Most often when we follow our hearts we are not disappointed. Our heart will lead us to look for the good in others and ourselves. Our heart will help us find our soul mate. Our heart will encourage us to help those less fortunate.

If you have not read the book "What Would Jesus Do?" may I suggest you do so? This book really gets you to think about how every action you take will cause a reaction for yourself as well as for others. When you follow your heart you will most often make the wisest choice.

When our heart feels good we feel good! Follow Your Heart, it will often take you places your mind will not allow you to go!

"It's not how much smarts you have, it's how much heart you have."

~James Malinchak

27

Don't Ever Say "Can't"

As a parent it really bothered me when one of my sons would say, "I can't do this." My response would always be, "How do you know you can't do it, until you have tried!" When pursuing your dreams and goals it's ever so important to think about ways YOU CAN do something rather than focusing on what you can't do!

Whenever I am faced with a challenge I quickly recite a variation of Philippians 4:13, "I can do all things through Christ, who strengthens me." Almost immediately after repeating this to myself several times I find strength to embrace the obstacle of setback I was facing!

Beginning today take the "t" out of can't and say, "I CAN!"

"Whether you think you can or can't, you are right."

~Henry Ford

28

Do What You Love and Love What You Do!

Many people follow in the footsteps of other family members and discover they are frustrated and disappointed with their lives because they are not doing what they want to do. They are living someone else's dream. Our parents, our peers, our teachers and professors can help us to discover what's right for us but ultimately if you are not doing what YOU LOVE you will never be working because you want to, you will be working because you need to.

Explore your options. Discover what you love to do. Let who you are, help you decide what to do! It's been said, "When you love what you do you'll never work another day in your life!" Choose to live your life on purpose!'

> *"Don't aim for success if you want it; just do what you love and believe in, and it will come naturally."*
>
> ~David Frost

29

Don't Waste Time

There are 1440 minutes in every day and the more minutes you can account for when you are working the more minutes you will have left over to play! When you work for someone else you are told what time to show up and how long you must stay. You have tasks you must get done and you may find yourself working during lunch breaks or taking work home if you don't get it done. Make a pledge to yourself to be as productive as you can during the day so you can accomplish what needs to be done in the allotted time.

If you are an entrepreneur and you create your own schedule it's important to schedule tasks at the time when you are most likely to be able to complete them. Most entrepreneurs find it's easier to do creative stuff in the morning when their mind is fresh and other mundane tasks that need to be done later in the day! Entrepreneurs need to remember, if it's not bringing in money it's probably not the most important thing to be doing right now!

Get into the habit of creating your schedule for the following day before you go to bed each night. When you begin work you will have your day planned and you'll soon discover you are accomplishing more in less time!

"Time is money."

~Benjamin Franklin

30

Have Faith In Yourself

In the early 1990's I invested in Tony Robbins, "Personal Power" program and I listened to the cassettes over and over again. I also took time to do the action steps along the way including the one where I had to write down a list of my goals. Year after year I checked off the things on my goal list until there was one goal left to complete. I wasn't quite ready to take the first step toward reaching that goal because the time was not right, so I put the notebook away for several years.

Then after the terrorist attack on September 11, 2001 I really got to thinking about my life and if I had really accomplished all I wanted to do! I realized I had one last thing on my goal list from 10 years earlier and that was to become a motivational speaker. Sooner or later I had to take the first step! My sons were grown so I would not feel guilty leaving them, and so after many heart-to-heart talks with my husband Larry I decided to take a leap of faith. I transferred my sales team to my up line leader and began to pursue the next phase of my life. I was more frightened by the unknown than I remember feeling anytime during my life but I'm happy to say I have never looked back!

"Faith is taking the first step even when you don't see the whole staircase."
~Martin Luther King Jr.

31

Don't Just Talk About it, DO IT!

Having been a sales leader for over twenty years I learned there are many people who dream and talk about doing things but never get "around to it." You'll hear people say, "I'm going to do this and I'm going to do that" and twenty years later they haven't done anything!

At one of our meetings my leader passed out a wooden coin to everyone and on the coin it said "tuit". She then told us, "Now all of you have a round tuit to remind you to do what you say you are going to do!"

It sounds kind of corny but if we really thought about all the things we say we are going to do that we never do we would have a list a mile long. If you find yourself continually talking about doing things but never taking the first step it's time to discover why? Are your fears holding you back? Are you afraid of trying something new? Are you someone who is content to just dream your life away without taking any action? Asking yourself questions and answering them honestly is the first step toward taking action!

Ready, set, GO!

"It's not the things you talk about doing that count, it's what you do that will determine your results."

~Karen Phelps

32

Keep Trying New Things

If you keep trying new things you will never run out of options. I must admit I am a junkie when it comes to trying out new things or new techniques. I'm not sure how long I have been like this but I know back when I was in sales I was always one of the first to try out a new idea. I am a doer and I don't want to waste time analyzing how or why an idea or technique might work I just want to try it as quickly as possible to see if it does.

This works well for me and often I will quickly find solutions to problems that arise. For every problem there are usually many different solutions. The secret is to uncover as many as possible and begin to try them out until you find the one that works for you!

You may be a thinker who has to evaluate, investigate, and explore every option before you make a decision to act. This may work well for you once in awhile; but you may often find yourself left in the dust by the doers! Find the balance that works well for you and do your best to try new ideas, techniques or things as soon as you get a chance.

"It only takes one great idea to get you back on track."

~Karen Phelps

33

Don't Settle
for Mediocrity

Are you excited to get up each morning to begin your day? Having a life purpose means you know who you want to become in the process of growing up! Living your life "on purpose" will help you do things that are in alignment with who you want to become and what you want to accomplish. Living your life "on purpose" will also help you to avoid people, places, things and habits that will not help you achieve your ultimate goal.

Ask yourself these 3 questions: Am I going where I want to go? Am I being who I want to be? Am I doing what I want to do? Once you have answered these 3 questions honestly and you begin to make decisions based on your desired results you will begin to become the meaningful specific God intended for you to be.

"When you discover your mission, you will feel its demand. It will fill you with enthusiasm and a burning desire to get to work on it."

~W. Clement Stone

Never Stop Learning

"It's what you learn after you know it all that counts."
John Wooden

When you are out of school, college or the university your learning should not stop there. Once you think you know it all, there is always something to learn. It has been said you can tell how smart a person is by the size of their library. How often do you read? Hey, you're reading this book so it's a start!

If you are not already in the habit of reading it's not too late to begin. You can read novels, biographies, auto-biographies, self-help books, and about things you would like to learn to do or things you know how to do but would like to get better at.

I have a colleague Alan Weiss who says, "I'm constantly amazed at how stupid I was yesterday." Every day offers you a new opportunity to do something or learn something new, but only if you keep your mind open and decide to remain a student. You'll be amazed at how smart and well-rounded people will think you are once you begin your never-ending quest for improvement in all areas of your life.

"Your ability to learn faster than your competition is your only sustainable competitive advantage."

~Ari Du Gues

35

Make Adjustments to Stay on Track

If you've ever sailed a boat you know that you must make constant adjustments in the sails if you want to stay on course. It is impossible to begin your excursion with the sails set one way and not make an adjustment in order to return to your destination.

The pursuit of your goals is like setting off on a sailing trip. You may reach one milestone on the way to your goal and then you discover you have to make a few adjustments in your action plan so that you can stay on track. When you are avidly pursuing your goals, evaluate and create an action plan, take action, re-evaluate and keep making adjustments along the way. Very rarely will you find your original action plan taking you all the way to the end!

"Greatness is not in where we stand, but in what direction we are moving. We must sail sometimes with the wind and sometimes against it - but sail we must and not drift, nor lie at anchor."

~Oliver Wendell Holmes

36

Quit Worrying

It's often easier to worry about something that may happen than it is to do something to prevent it. Worries are fears that position themselves in our minds and continue to grow as we feed them with more and more thoughts of what "might happen." When you focus on the "worst possible outcome" over and over in your mind you begin to believe these things will come to pass.

People worry about their health and yet worry is one of the quickest ways to destroy your health. The first time your child attends school you worry about what may happen when he or she is out of your sight and when they return home you discover nothing happened. We worry what will happen to our job, to our marriage, to our family and about so many other things that the worry eventually prevents us from taking any kind of action.

There is only one way to happiness and that is to cease worrying about things which are beyond our control. According to one of my favorite songs by Bobby McFerrin, "In every life we have some trouble, but when you worry you make it double, DON'T WORRY...BE HAPPY!"

"Worry will not put you closer to your goals it will only put more obstacles in your way."
~Karen Phelps

37

Treat Every Day as a Gift

Each morning when we awake we are adding a new day to our lives. The day will pass and we will never get those 24 hours back again. They are gone forever. Make sure you do all you can each day for you never know if you will get another.

Each new day you are given a brand new opportunity to do what you did not get done yesterday, or the day before that, or the day before that. You have another chance to heal a broken relationship. You have another chance to give thanks for all your blessings. You have another chance to spend some quality time with your family. You have another chance to complete a project. You have another chance to do anything you want to do!

Each new day is a new opportunity to make it your best day ever! Treat each day as the truly special gift it is.

"This is the day the Lord has made, let us rejoice and be glad in it."

~Psalm 118:24

38

Don't Let Anyone
Rain on Your Parade

It's easy for others to squash our dreams and tell us what we can or cannot have. Dump them! Get them out of your life! Being around negative people is like getting stuck in quicksand; it's hard to get out! The more negative people you are surrounded by the less chance you have of accomplishing what you want in life. You have to remove yourself from these people. You need to decide not to listen to their negativity.

Don't let anyone tell you that you can't do something or be someone, it's not their decision, IT'S YOURS! What others tell you is not important, it's what you tell yourself that will help you reach your goals.

The sooner you begin to hang around positive people the sooner your life will become better!

The positive results on your business and your future will be worth the effort!

"No one can make you feel inferior without your consent."

~Eleanor Roosevelt

39

Do Everything
with Enthusiasm

Enthusiasm comes from the Greek word "enthios" which means "the god within". Think back to when you've been excited and enthusiastic about something. Did your enthusiasm provide you with an energy that kept you motivated and moving?

You need enthusiasm to be successful in all areas of your life. Enthusiasm is the outward display of our inner passion! Enthusiasm carries us far beyond what our skills and talents can carry us. You've seen rookies in your industry outsell the pros when they had "very little knowledge" but a "ton of enthusiasm". Enthusiasm brings out the drive in us. It helps us reach our goals.

"Without enthusiasm you are a little fish in a big sea. Add enthusiasm and you become a BIG SHARK ready to destroy all obstacles in your way."

~Karen Phelps

40

Slow Down

I sometimes feel like my life is whirling past me and I need to stop and slow it down! Every year I was in direct selling I earned a free trip and I used those trips to slow down and take time to renew my spirit.

Taking a vacation is one of my favorite ways to slow down and just get centered. Larry and I make sure we schedule vacation time every year. My idea of a perfect vacation is relaxing by the pool with a novel and I judge how relaxing my vacation was by how many novels I am able to read. My record was 11 books in 2 weeks!

It may be impossible to take a vacation every week but that doesn't mean you can't take some time to slow down. Take a walk, relax in the hammock (I'm still waiting for this one), read a magazine, watch a romantic movie or take a nap! Your work will still be there when you come back but you will feel renewed and ready to tackle the world when you take time to unwind.

"The time to relax is when you don't have time for it."

~Sidney J. Harris

41

Have a Compassionate Heart

When you think of compassionate people certainly Mother Theresa is one of the first to come to mind as she did so much to not only help the poor but to bring attention to their plight. In my life my mother was one of the most compassionate people I have known. She helped whenever she was needed even if it was not convenient for her or our family. When I was young she took in a woman and her three children in order to get them away from an abusive husband and father. Though our family already had nine mouths to feed she made it work until other arrangements could be found.

I think it was then I truly discovered what a truly amazing person my mother was. After that I began to tune into the ways my mom was there to help others. Through watching her I soon discovered ways I could do things to help others too! There is always someone who needs a helping hand, encouragement or a hug. Sometimes it's as simple as being there when someone needs you.

"Compassion makes the world a better place. The quickest way to forget your troubles is to help someone who has less than you."
~Karen Phelps

42

Let Your Actions Speak Louder Than Your Words

I'm sure you have heard the cliché, "Your actions are so loud I can't hear a word you are saying." Do you let your words or your actions speak for you? Do you tell your children not to smoke and drink with a cigarette in one hand and a beer in the other? Are your actions congruent with what you say?

The best way to raise a family is to be a constant role model for the type of person you want them to become. Living your life with love, honesty, and compassion is easier than telling them to love their neighbors, always tell the truth, and to do good for others.

Be mindful that your words and your actions are in alignment with each other.

> *"Children more attention pay, to what you do than what you say."*
>
> ~Zig Ziglar

43

Always Be Yourself

A lady came up to me after I spoke at her company's convention and she said, "Do you know what I like about you?" Somewhat surprised I asked, "What?" She replied, "I like that you are comfortable in your own skin. You know what you stand for and you aren't afraid to let people know."

There are times when I have felt that I might be coming across too tough in a newsletter I am writing, or during coaching with a client. Then I get an email from someone who says, "Your newsletter was just what I needed to hear." Or, the coaching client tells me, "What you said to me made such a difference. I am now getting much more done in much less time."

I once made the comment at an event I was putting on that I was going to try to tone it down a little; the group of people I was speaking to immediately said, "Don't. That's what we like about you. You hold us accountable. You don't sugar coat stuff. You tell it like it is! DON'T CHANGE!" And so I won't!

Be proud of who you are and what you stand for! Be Unique! BE YOU!

"What you see, is what you get!"
~Flip Wilson, Laugh-In

44

Be Happy

Only you can take control of your own happiness. Don't rely on other people to make you happy. Don't rely on things to make you happy.

The first time I watched the Walt Disney movie, Snow White and the Seven Dwarf I didn't like Grumpy much because he was always complaining. I remember thinking I want to be like Happy!

Let the little things in life make you happy. A beautiful sunrise, a perfect flower, holding a baby in your arms, a happy song and a comedy are just a few of the things that make me happy. Happiness is an attitude! Happiness is a choice. You are as happy as you want to be!

"A happy person is not a person in a certain set of circumstances, but rather a person with a certain set of attitudes."
~Hugh Downs

45

Don't Let the Urgent Replace the Important

I am constantly working to meet deadlines. I have a never-ending pile of work on my desk and I could easily work my life away. But, I won't. I won't because even though there are many urgent things that need to be done there are many important things I want to do!

We can all live in crisis mode if we want to! You have to choose not to. If you find that everything on your list is urgent you might want to take a good look at things. Do you have too many things on your list? Can some of the tasks be delegated? Can some things on your list be dropped? Can some of them be done later? Do you put things off so long everything becomes urgent? If that's the case, Brian Tracy's book, "Eat that Frog" will help you learn to prioritize your list.

Do you know what's important to you? Can you list several times when you missed something important because you had to do something else? Only you can make the decision to do the important things first. Trust me... the urgent will always be there!

"Things which matter most must never be at the mercy of things which matter least."
~Johann Wolfgang Von Goethe

46

Family and Friends Come First

My mom always made family a priority and that quality has been passed down from generation to generation. We gather frequently to hang out with each other, celebrate birthdays and special occasions and just laugh and have fun. My six siblings and I started a tradition several years ago. Every year we go away for a weekend with no spouses and it's always a lot of fun. We share stories from when we were young, we solve the problems of the world and YES there are some occasional spats. But when the weekend is over we are renewed in our love for each other.

Even though my life gets crazy, there is always time for family dinners, grandparent's days and of course date nights with my husband. I also set aside one night a month for girlfriend night and meet my friends for dinner and to enjoy each other's company. There is so much fun and laughter that I feel renewed in mind and spirit when I come home. When I am really busy I sometimes think about skipping my night out to get work done, then I think to myself, "I deserve to have some fun with my friends" and I go and have a great time!

Nurture your relationships for they are important for the soul. Spend time with your parents, grandparents, children, grandchildren, brothers and sisters, nieces and nephews and friends for the time you spend with them will be shorter than you think. When they are gone it will not be the time spent with them you regret but the times you were too busy to care.

"To us, family means putting your arms around each other and being there."

~Barbara Bush

47

Don't Be
Afraid of Change

Change is scary. Change is good! Change can well…
change your life! How you view change will determine
how successful and fulfilled you become both profession-
ally and personally. You cannot expect to go through your
life without making changes so look at each change as an
opportunity to grow.

If you were doing a certain task one way and you knew
there was another way that would not only be faster but
would produce better results what would you do? Would
you change to the new way as soon as possible or would
you be hesitant and only change if and when you were
forced to? People who avoid change are often stuck in a
rut and can't or won't get out of it!

Your ability to adapt to change will continually move
you in the direction of your goals! One of my favorite
quotes is listed below and was from the President of the
company I was in for many years. I believe it says it all!

*"Things are the way you like them or else
you'd change."*

~John Frederick

48

Be an Inspiration for Others

For me being an inspiration means being someone who inspires others to be better, do more or try something new. I was a direct selling leader for twenty-five years and one of my goals was to inspire each member of my team to be the best they can be. I trained my team, I coached each member and I encouraged each of them to define their reasons for wanting their business to succeed.

Most of us can trace our success back to someone who was an inspiration in our life. It may have been a loving and supportive parent, a teacher who took a little extra time, a coach who showed you how to improve your game, or a combination of many influential people who helped mold you into the person you now are.

It's now time to give back. Encourage others to be the best they can be! Be the light that shows the way!

"If your actions inspire others to dream more, learn more, do more and become more, you are a leader."
~John Quincy Adams

49

Be Thankful

Each night when I go to bed and many times during the day I take a few minutes to thank God for all the blessings in my life. There are many people who have much more than I have BUT there are millions of people who have a lot less.

When you learn to be thankful you will begin to remove the focus from what you don't have to what you do have in your life. Be thankful for your life, for your health, for your family, for the roof over your head and the food on your table. Be thankful that you live in a Country that allows you the freedom to choose who and what you want to become. Be thankful that you can believe in the God of your choice. There is a never-ending list of things to be thankful for and those who choose to live a life of abundance will always look for the blessings in their life.

Develop the habit of giving thanks for the abundance in your life and don't be surprised when more good things come your way!

"Let us rise up and be thankful, for if we didn't learn a lot today, at least we learned a little, and if we didn't learn a little, at least we didn't get sick, and if we got sick, at least we didn't die; so, let us all be thankful."
~Buddha

50

Live Your Life to the Fullest

Live your life with gusto! Live your life with no regrets! Live your life on purpose! Try everything you want to try, do everything you want to do, don't let your fears hold you back.

Your willingness is the key that unlocks life's abundance. Be willing to learn and a teacher will appear. Be willing to work and opportunities will come your way. Be willing to love and people will be attracted to you. Be willing to laugh at yourself and you will never be afraid of making mistakes. Be willing to live your life to the fullest and you will never have any regrets!

"When I stand before God at the end of my life, I would hope that I would not have a single bit of talent left, and could say, I used everything you gave me."

~Erma Bombeck

A Note from the Author

I believe we all were created to be the best we can be! I've just shared with you some principles that I live by to help me in all facets of my business and life. No one can think for you. No one can do the work for you. No one can tell you how to feel! YOU and only YOU are in control of every aspect of your life.

There are no guarantees that your life will be perfect and that you will have success beyond your wildest imagination. However, I believe if you begin to implement some of these simple tips you can begin living a more fulfilled life and you will move closer and closer to your dreams and goals.

Today is the day to decide to be better than you were yesterday! Today is the first day of the rest of your life! Make it amazing! Make it wonderful! You Can Do It!

Take the next step toward getting more in your life by checking out the success products available at:

www.karenphelps.com